The Wisdom of the East

EDITED BY J. L. CRANMER-BYNG M.C.

AN ESSAY ON LANDSCAPE PAINTING

This edition is distributed in the U.S.A. by Grove Press Inc.,
795 Broadway, New York 3, N.Y.

AN ESSAY ON LANDSCAPE PAINTING

(*LIN CH'ÜAN KAU CHIH*)

KUO HSI

Translated by

SHIO SAKANISHI

John Murray
Fifty Albemarle Street
London

First published 1935
Reprinted 1936
Reprinted 1949
Reprinted 1959

Printed in Great Britain
by Butler & Tanner Ltd.,
Frome and London

To

DeWitt Henry Parker

My Teacher and Friend

Editorial Note

The object of the Editor of this series is a very definite one. He desires above all things that these books shall be the ambassadors of good-will between East and West. He hopes that they will contribute to a fuller knowledge of the great cultural heritage of the East, for only through real understanding will the West be able to appreciate the underlying problems and aspirations of Asia to-day. He is confident that a deeper knowledge of the great ideals and lofty philosophy of Eastern thought will help to a revival of that true spirit of charity which neither despises nor fears the nations of another creed and colour.

J. L. CRANMER-BYNG

50 Albemarle Street
London, W.1

Contents

Foreword

Sung Culture and Ideals,
A.D. *960–1279*

Nearly a thousand years ago a great and ancient people whose outlook on life was based on the law of rhythm and the duality of Nature through the Yin and Yang (the female and male principle) entered upon its Golden Age. It is impossible to discuss the Sung or any other period of Chinese culture without reference to the religious ideals of the Chinese sages and the sacred classics. From the earliest beginnings there was a Way both spiritual and national to be trodden by all. It was called *Tao* and there have been many interpretations of this most elusive word, each one giving some particular aspect of a thought too vast to be encompassed. There are three Tao—the Tao of Heaven or Tí'en Tao, the Tao of Earth or T'i Tao, and the union of the two produces the Tao of Man or Jen Tao. In the *Book of Rites*, called *Li Chi*, one of the Five Classics, we read—'Man is a product of the beneficial operation of Heaven and Earth.'

There is again the Tao of Confucius the rationalist and social reformer, and the Tao of Lao-tzŭ the idealist and individualist. The first corresponds to the spirit of

Northern China, the second to the Southern spirit. From the days of Confucius and Lao-tzŭ up to the time of the Mings, about A.D. 1421, the whole of Chinese history bears witness to the struggle between the two rival forces. When both were equally balanced the Empire flourished, when either prevailed it weakened and decay set in. Under the Mings Confucianism finally prevailed and the history of China follows a slow downward course only relieved by slight upward curves during the reigns of the two great Manchu Emperors K'ang Hsi and Ch'ien Lung.

In dealing with Sung culture and ideals it is difficult to make any hard and fast distinction between Confucianist and Taoist. T'ai Tsu, the founder of the Sung dynasty, gave a certain impetus to Confucianism when he revived the literary examination tests, based upon the Confucian Classics, for all administrative posts. Had literature occupied the predominant position it had attained under the previous dynasty of T'ang the result might have been very different. But already the epoch of great writers was drawing to its close. Two names alone stand out to challenge comparison with the poets of the T'ang—Ou-yang Hsiu and Su Tung-po. The giants of literature have shrunk to little more than men in the dawn of the Sung, which is also the dawn of the greatest pictorial art the East has ever known. And other influences and ideals than those of Confucius inspired the artists of that day. Chinese Taoism and Indian Buddhism profoundly modified by its contact with native thought are the parents of Sung art. 'A man's religion,' says Tolstoi, 'is the relation which he believes himself to bear to the endless universe around him, and to the source of that endless universe.' And the first essential of a living religion is surely an inner sense of values linking us with the great reality in which we are contained. Only in naturalness and simplicity of spirit can we make contact with that which is both origin and goal.

'I hold it is better to have the true ease of spiritual culture than the sweets of Empire. It is better to roam in the infinitude of naturalness and have a true apprehension of the relationship between the visible and the invisible than to have the pleasure of glory and renown. To possess a well-ordered life and have a logical apprehension of Being and non-Being is the great thing.

'Universal praise adds no encouragement to such a man, nor would there be any abatement of purpose, even were the whole realm to be hostile. These men have a clear and definite idea of the value of life and death, and a clear perception of what constitutes honour and shame.' [1]

Thus it is not the doctrines that we propound and

[1] *Tao, the Great Luminant*, by Evan Morgan, p. 48. London, Kegan Paul.

impose on others but our whole attitude towards Life from source to goal that matters. This vision of a well-ordered life brings us back to rhythm, for life is manifest in movement and rhythm is the controlled flow of movement. 'Deeper than all the rhythm of art,' says the writer of the article on Poetry in the *Encyclopædia Britannica*, 'is that rhythm that art would fain catch, the rhythm of life itself. . . . Being rhythm it is of course governed by law, but it is a law which transcends in subtlety the conscious art of the metricist . . . a law which, being part of Nature's own sanctions, can . . . never be formulated but only expressed, as it is in the melody of a bird.'

Towards the end of the fifth century A.D. Hsieh Ho, 'the first systematic writer on art', and consequently the forerunner of Kuo Hsi, wrote his celebrated Six Canons of Art. The last five are concerned with method and technique and therefore chiefly interesting to art students. But the first Canon is of deepest significance since it contains the whole philosophy underlying Chinese art. It has been variously translated by Herbert Giles, Okakura, and Laurence Binyon as follows:

Rhythmic Vitality, or Spiritual Rhythm expressed in the movement of life.

Or the Life-movement of the Spirit through the rhythm of things.

Or the fusion of the rhythm of the Spirit with the movement of living things.

But as Mr Binyon points out, 'what is certainly meant is that the artist must pierce beneath the mere aspect of the world to seize and himself be possessed by that great cosmic rhythm of the spirit which sets the currents of life in motion'.[1]

Thus the great achievement of the Chinese artist 'is to fuse the spiritual and the material'. Yet according to the Taoist there is no dead and lifeless matter since the divine energy of Tao permeates all. The activities of the humblest things are hidden; it is the duty of the artist to bring them to light, to transmute them as a potter transmutes clay, by mixing, by the use of the potter's wheel, by coloured glazes and by firing. But if he does not love his material neither can he work on it. Rhythm seeks rhythm and both combine to produce one harmony. And if rhythm is the creative law of life then 'love is the fulfilling of the law'. Here it is the Tao of Man responding to the Tao of Earth.

Late in the T'ang period Buddhism in its new aspect and fusion with Taoism, known as Zen, enters, bringing man and Nature into closer contact 'through direct communion with the inner nature of things'. Okakura, in *The Book of Tea*, has told us that 'A special contribution of Zen to Eastern thought was its recognition of

[1] *The Flight of the Dragon*, pp. 13 and 14.

the mundane as of equal importance with the spiritual. It held that in the great relation of things there was no distinction of small or great, an atom possessing equal possibilities with the universe.' The outcome of this teaching was apparent in the Zen monastery where the least action, the most menial service had to be done perfectly. So 'Taoism furnished the basis for æsthetic ideals, Zennism made them practical'. But the influence of both religions and their meaning for us is shown above all in the pictorial and ceramic art of the Sung. Every vase and beaker in the Eumorfopoulos Collection is a living object, a thing of beauty and a joy for ever. And in the later Ming period hints of symbolism, legend and the lore of a vanished world are coloured like figures in half-told tales round the circumference of a porcelain bowl where the master's impenetrable glaze has hushed them in. They are not dead but *poised.* All human rhythm expressed in life, in poetry, in art, in music ends in poise. The great life that was lived in its fullness, the great work of art, finished so far as its creator is concerned, stays poised. The spirit of Li Lung-mien is poised in the Western Garden where he painted himself and his fifteen contemporaries, Buddhists, Taoists and Confucianists, poets, statesmen and painters, the united forces of Sung culture in its prime. For what after all is poise but the antithesis of inertia, the zenith of movement, the challenge to oblivion, and the triumph of man over destiny. Life centred around Kai-feng-fu, the capital of the Northern Sung, and after its capture by the Nü-chên Tartars around Hangchow was in some ways the nearest approach to Heaven on Earth the world has known as yet. A nation of artists, artisans and nature worshippers was drawn together by a common bond and a common aim in living creatively, each one intent on his own work, conscious of the joy that creation brings yet greatly aware in his hours of leisure of the supreme happiness that can only be partaken in communion. And as I have pointed out in *The Vision of Asia*,[1] 'With the Chinese communion is not with some small section of one's fellow-worshippers at a particular shrine, not even with humanity, but with life in every aspect; not with contemporary life alone, but with a living past and a future that widens its avenues and horizons to receive us.'

Perhaps, after all, T'ai Tsu was wiser than he knew when he made administrators of young literary men and scholars. It brought both literature and scholarship into touch with life and after much chastening when the scholar learnt to 'temper his harshness' and the literary man to 'moderate his brilliancy' there emerged a leader of the people trained in the wholesome discipline of public affairs with a fuller

[1] *The Vision of Asia*, pp. 181, 182. London, John Murray.

understanding of the values of leisure. Such a leader was the Confucian Su Tung-p'o, poet and provincial governor, architect and engineer. In the endless quarrels between the followers of Confucius and those of Lao-tzŭ it was urged by the former that their opponents despised all learning and knowledge. Nothing could be further from the truth. What the Taoist objected to, and rightly, was the attitude of Chuange Tzŭ's frog in a well to whom it was useless to speak of the ocean. The scholar who remained merely a scholar in the midst of life was the ultra conservative who could see no good in the present and no evil in the past, the type of man who drove reformers out of office and emperors from their thrones. Being self-centred he was unadaptable and adaptability is a chief essential in the affairs of men. As for knowledge for the sake of knowledge, the Taoist would say in effect, 'You know something? Then make a song, a dance, a silken robe of it. But please refrain from sweeping the room with your sleeves.' In the end the Confucian scholar brought the Empire to the dust and has succeeded ever since in covering the annals of a great country with the dust of scholarship.

But sufficient of the art of the Sung remains to show how vast it was, and how sublime in its spirituality. Compare it with the art of any other people and it is still beyond them, unchallengeable by all.

For, as Mrs Wingate has pointed out: 'The Chinese

ideal alone remains entirely spiritual, because it is unaffected by any human desire to improve it. His design may be elaborate, but so may be the design of Nature. The difference between man-made elaborization and natural elaborization is that one is haphazard and the other is exact; the one excites the sense, the other satisfies it; the one distracts the eye, the other fills it and gives it rest.

'To the Chinese mind . . . Nature itself is symbolical. All creation typifies something higher, and the clearer the design the more apparent the purpose.' [1]

With such an outlook on the Universe it is small wonder that the Sung artist delighted in landscape above all other subjects. What he really expresses is the meeting and union of two characters—the character of Man. Never did the artist approach Nature without reverence and preparation. Of Kuo Hsi his son tells us something of his father's method of approach.[2]

The spirits of Kuo Hsi and his great contemporaries Li Lung-mien, the Emperor Hui Tsung, who established the first Academy of Painting, Ma Yüan of the Southern Sung, the Buddhist priest Mu Ch'i are free spirits roaming the Universe at will yet acknowledging in all reverence the control of Li or Universal Law.

[1] *The Golden Phœnix, Essays on Chinese Art and Culture,* by Mrs Alfred Wingate, p. 38. London, Herbert Jenkins.

[2] See p. 37.

Foreword

The profound yet humble vision of China's seers and sages taught them that religion is the tree of which art is the blossom and wisdom the fruit, that the good life is one which reveals at its close beauty matured as wisdom. That is why all China paid homage to old age. It also taught them their place in Nature, not as lords of creation or petty tyrants despoiling and defiling, but as members of the Fellowship of Life.

L. Cranmer-Byng

Preface

Kuo Hsi's *Essay on Landscape Painting* has been read for centuries by Chinese and Japanese artists and has been extremely influenced in shaping the course of the later schools of landscape painting. It is made up of the sayings of Kuo Hsi to his son, who after his father's death put them into their present form. The essay falls into four sections: Comments on Landscapes; The Meaning of Painting; Rules for Painting; a Supplement to the Rules for Painting. To the last is appended another very short section consisting of a few anecdotes about Kuo Hsi's work; it has no connection with the essay proper. In the present translation the fourth section has been omitted, because critics agree that it is an interpolation of a very much later period.

The translation is based on the two Chinese editions of the 'Lin Ch'üan Kao Chih': in the *Wang Shih Hua Yüan* and the *Mei Shu Ts'ung Shu*; and a short extract in the *Hua Hsüeh Hsin Yin*. I have consulted a complete Japanese translation and several partial translations in English and French. To these works I refer students who are interested in the variant interpretations of the more doubtful passages:

IMAZEKI, HISAMARO. *Tôyô garon shûsei* (A Collection of Essays on Oriental Painting), Vol. I, pp. 43–63. Tokyo, 1916.

SIRÉN, OSVALD. *A History of Early Chinese Painting*, Vol. 2, pp. 9–25. London, 1933.

FENOLLOSA, ERNEST FRANCISCO. *Epochs of Chinese and Japanese Art*, Vol. 2, pp. 10–19. New York, 1921.

WALEY, ARTHUR. *An Introduction to the Study of Chinese Painting*, pp. 189–194. London, 1923.

PETRUCCI, R. 'Morceaux choisis d'esthétique', *Osrasiat. Zeitschrift*, Vol. 1, No 4, Jan. 1915, pp. 395–400.

GILES, HERBERT A. *An Introduction to the History of Chinese Pictorial Art*, pp. 114–17. London, 1918.

I am deeply indebted to Mr. L. Cranmer-Byng for the suggestion that I should translate the essay of Kuo Hsi. Without his constant encouragement I should not have had the courage to complete this difficult task. I wish to thank George Kennedy for looking over the Preface and the two opening paragraphs of the text, and Tomoo Numata for many helpful corrections and suggestions. A grateful acknowledgment is due to Lilian E. Knowles for assisting me in the final revision of the manuscript.

S. S.

LIBRARY OF CONGRESS,
June 8, 1935.

Note.—The Editors desire to express their indebtedness to the Prints Department of the British Museum for allowing them to reproduce a contemporary drawing as the cover design.

Introduction

Kuo Hsi, whose *tzŭ* was Shun-fu, was born in Honan Province about 1020. Of his parents and of his early education we know practically nothing. A few phrases in the *Preface to An Essay on Landscape Painting* written by his son Kuo Jo-hsü tell us that he followed the teachings of Lao-tzŭ, and that before him there were no traditions of painting in the family. We also know, from a statement in the *Hsüan Ho Hua P'u*, that he was admitted at an early age to the Imperial Academy of Painting and soon made himself known for his bold and masterly brush-work. If we may be permitted to reconstruct his later history from other scattered notes, we may state with some certainty that in middle life he acquired great fame as a landscape painter, for he was called to the court to paint large frescoes on the walls of the Imperial Palace. Later still he became a member of the Imperial Council and held various honorary offices.

By his contemporaries Kuo Hsi was considered the greatest master of his day. He had early been attracted to the work of Li Ch'êng, one of the most important landscape artists of the early Northern Sung dynasty.

Throughout his life Li Ch'êng was to him a source of inspiration. His own theory of artistic training as expressed in his *Essay* prevented him, however, from following too closely the work of any one master. The palace frescoes undoubtedly represented his most ambitious work. They embodied, we know, in theme and execution the principles laid down in the *Essay*. Unfortunately later on in the Sung dynasty, when the æsthetic ideals of the Emperors reverted once more to those of the Han and T'ang periods, his frescoes were whitewashed and his series of great landscapes, which had been hung in the palace halls, was taken down to be lost in oblivion.

In the collection of the Palace Museum in Peiping there is a great hanging scroll, *Early Spring* (*Tsao Ch'un*), signed and dated by Kuo Hsi in the year which corresponds to 1072. So far as we can judge from the few extant works attributed to him, this is one of his masterpieces, a painting which probably consummates a long period of effort and preparation. The scroll is a worthy representative of the work of an artist renowned for his remarkable skill and imaginative power. Osvald Sirén writes of it:

> The details are infinitesimal, the forms and shapes of endless variation, but they are all woven into a great winding movement that dominates the main part of the picture; only the crowning peaks are straight and quiet. None of

the earlier masters could bring a great and exuberantly rich motive so completely under the domination of a unifying rhythm and remould it so freely in accordance with an expressionistic idea.

Kuo Hsi's *Essay* speaks for itself. His predecessors, Ku K'ai-chih, Ching Hao, and others, had set down in their fragmentary treatises abstract theories on the art of landscape painting, and he follows in their footsteps. His discussion, however, is more thorough than theirs; his application of general theories is at once more practical and more personal. The primary contribution of the *Essay* to the study of æsthetics, however, lies not in its technical advice—which is indeed excellent in itself—but in its presentation of a thoroughly integrated conception of the essential spirituality of all art. He defines the purpose of landscape painting, demands that it shall supply the beholder with an imagined scene to take the place of a desired objective reality. He recommends an eclectic method of study: the artist must know well the best that has been done; must master many different kinds of technique. In time he will have subdued to his purposes all the conventions of perspective and arrangement which are the means of artistic expression. Finally he will succeed in establishing a style of his own. Kuo Hsi expects that style to arise from the artist's comprehension of the essential quality, character, or significance of his subject.

This the artist can grasp only if his spirit is untroubled and free. This the artist can express only at the cost of intense mental energy and severe mental discipline. So the art of painting is to Kuo Hsi a manifestation of the artist's power to comprehend and express the spiritual reality of concrete natural objects.

The literary style of the *Essay* is one of extreme balance, balance of thought as well as of phrase. Repetitions and parallelisms which seem absurd in English prose fall with precise fitness into the highly artificial scheme of the Chinese form and arouse in the expectant minds of those who read in the original that sense of felicity and aptness which English readers know best in the antithetical, balanced niceties of a couplet by Dryden or Pope. It was extremely difficult to preserve that balance in this translation. Too often, indeed, the arrangement could not be transferred, or it lost in the transference its original fitness and beauty.

Finally Kuo Hsi uses some phrases whose meaning is no longer intelligible, the very sources of which are now lost.

An Essay on Landscape Painting

(Lin Ch'üan Kao Chih)

Preface

By Kuo Jo-hsü

It is said in the *Analects*: ''Tis well to aim at the moral principle *Tao*, to derive authority in everything from virtue, to regulate the conduct by benevolence and to let the mind play in the sphere of art.' By art is meant ritual, music, archery, charioteering, calligraphy, and numbers. Calligraphy is a branch of painting. The *shan-fên*, the ch'i-fên, and the *hsing-fên* of the *Book of Changes* arise from the three essences.[1] *Shan* like the moutain, *ch'i* like the atmosphere, *hsing* like the form: these are the elements of painting. Huang-ti, the Yellow Emperor, had clothes made on which were put a certain number of insignia or a pattern, which in time became the basic motifs used in painting. Speaking of the twelve insignia of the Emperor Shun, in particular of the mountain, the dragon, and the brightly-coloured bird, he said: 'Note carefully the representations of the ancients.' The *Êrh-ya*, the earliest Chinese dictionary, says: 'Painting is representation', showing that representation develops into painting. In *Hsi-tz'ŭ*, the commentary on the statement in the *Book of Changes*, 'Note carefully the representations', the same development is implied. The statement in the *Analects* that 'the painting comes after the groundwork', and in the *Rites of Chou* that 'the work of colouring and painting comes after the groundwork has been laid', shows that the beginnings of skilful painting go back to remote antiquity. There is the ancient tradition that Fu Hsi[2] drew the eight trigrams, where the word 'drew' is taken in the sense which it has in the phrase 'Now you are limiting yourself' and is defined as synonymous with 'set a boundary to'. I do not, however, understand what would be the meaning of 'setting a boundary to the eight trigrams'.

On these grounds the character for 'to paint' should be written differently, but since painting, as we know it at present, arose in a later age, the modern form of the character alone is used. In the ancient forms of characters that have been preserved, birds and fish all appear in pictorial form. That is the method of painting by picturization.

When I was a little boy with pigtails, I followed my late father on wanderings among springs and rocks. Each time he put his brush to paper, he used to say: 'There is a method in landscape painting. How dare an artist paint in a careless manner?' Whenever I had listened to one of his opinions, I wrote it down immediately in my note-book. Now having collected several hundreds of these, I cannot let them slip into oblivion; therefore I present them to lovers of landscapes.

Strange to say, my father, who followed the teachings of Taoism in his youth, was inclined to abandon the old in his welcome of the new, and to live remote from conventional society. There was no tradition of painting in the family, and only his natural talent led him to give his fancy free play in the sphere of art and to make a name in it. Nevertheless, he was rich in inner character, in good deeds, in devotion to parents and friends, and in charity to all. In these he moved and had his being. These virtues of his should be known to his descendants.

Comments on Landscapes

(*Shan Shui Hsün*)

Why does a virtuous man take delight in landscapes? It is for these reasons: that in a rustic retreat he may nourish his nature; that amid the carefree play of streams and rocks, he may take delight; that he may constantly meet in the country fishermen, wood-cutters, and hermits, and see the soaring of the cranes, and hear the crying of the monkeys. The din of the dusty world and the locked-in-ness of human habitations are what human nature habitually abhors; while, on the contrary, haze, mist, and the haunting spirits of the mountains are what human nature seeks, and yet can rarely find. When, however, in the hey-day of great peace and prosperity, the minds, both of a man's sovereign and of his parents, are full of high expectations of his services, should he still stand aloof, neglecting the responsibilities of honour and righteousness? In the face of such duties the benevolent man cannot seclude himself and shun the world. He cannot hope to equal in spirit virtuous hermits such as Chi Tzŭ and Yin Hsü-yu or to share the good name of Hsia Huang-kung and Ch'i Li-chi.[3]

The ode entitled the 'White Colt' and the song of the 'Purple Plant' are gone for ever. Having no access to the landscapes, the lover of forest and stream, the friend of mist and haze, enjoys them only in his dreams. How delightful then to have a landscape painted by a skilled hand! Without leaving the room, at once, he finds himself among the streams and ravines; the cries of the birds and monkeys are faintly audible to his senses; light on the hills and reflection on the water, glittering, dazzle his eyes. Does not such a scene satisfy his mind and captivate his heart? That is why the world values the true significance of the painting of mountains. If this is not recognized, and the landscapes are roughly and carelessly approached, then is it not like spoiling a magnificent view and polluting the pure wind?

There are various ways of painting landscapes. They may be spread out in large compositions and yet contain nothing superfluous. They may be condensed to a small scene and yet lack nothing. There are also different ways of looking at landscapes. If one approaches them with the sympathetic spirit of a nature lover, their value is high; but if one approaches them with the eyes of pride and extravagance, their value is low.

Landscapes are large objects and he who looks at them must do so from a distance if he is to grasp the form, the position, the spirit, and the image of mountains and streams. As for paintings of men and women, made with small brush strokes, they can be held in the palm of the hand or readily unfurled to view on a small table, where they can be completely grasped in one glance. These are different manners of painting.

It is the considered judgment of mankind that there are landscapes in which one can travel, landscapes which can be gazed upon, landscapes in which one may ramble, and landscapes in which one may dwell. When any painting reaches one of these standards, it enters the category of the pre-excellent. However, one suitable for travelling in or gazing upon is not as successful as one in which one may dwell or ramble. Why is this? Look at the landscape paintings of to-day. They portray mountains and streams spread over the earth for several hundred miles. These are all accepted as suitable for living in or rambling in; yet only three- to four-tenths of the whole are deservedly so. Nevertheless these few beautiful landscapes arouse in the superior man a yearning for forest and stream. Therefore, the painters should work with this idea in mind, and the beholders should study the paintings with this same idea. This is what is meant by not losing sight of the fundamental idea.

Painting also has its laws of physiognomy. Li Ch'êng's[4] descendants were numerous and flourishing.

The foothills of his mountains were heavy and broad, elegant above and luxuriant below—an appropriate symbol of posterity. We deduce this conclusion not only from the laws of physiognomy; it is supported also by reason itself.

Learning to paint is no different from learning to write. With time one could imitate exactly the masterpieces of Chung Yu, Wang Hsi-chih, Yü Shih-nan, and Liu Kung-ch'üan. The great man and the virtuoso, however, will not limit himself to one school, but will cull and compare, discuss and investigate until he is able to establish his own school. Now the students of the Ch'i and Lu districts imitate only Li Ying-ch'iu, while the students of the Kuan and Shên imitate only Fan K'uan. They follow one path only, the steps of their predecessors, although their respective provinces comprise many thousand miles and contain a great many districts and kinds of people worthy of being represented. Narrow specialization has from ancient times been an evil. It is like harping on one note or playing on one string. Yet he who is unwilling to listen cannot blame one who does not listen. As experience testifies, man's eye and ear take delight in what is new and dislike what is old. This is the same the world over, and that is why I believe the great man and the virtuoso do not limit themselves to one school.

Liu Tzŭ-hou[5] often discussed the art of writing. To

me it seems that there is a principle not only in writing but also in everything. How much more should there be one in painting! Why do I say this? In painting a scene, irrespective of its size or scope, an artist should concentrate his spirit upon the essential nature of his work. If he fails to get at the esssential, he will fail to present the soul of his theme. Discipline should give his picture dignity. Without dignity depth is impossible. Diligence and reverence will make his work complete. Without that diligence it will remain incomplete.

Therefore when the artist is lazily forcing himself to work and is failing to draw from the very depths of his resources, then his painting is weak and soft and lacking in decisiveness. His fault is that of not concentrating on the essential. If he is confused and has cloudy ideas, then the forms become obscure and uncertain. His fault is that of not putting his whole soul into his work. If he approaches his painting too lightly, then the forms are likely to be disjointed and inharmonious. His fault is lack of dignity. If he neglects his work out of conceit, then the composition is careless and incomplete. His fault is lack of diligence. Therefore indecisiveness leads to faulty analysis, dullness to a lack of elegance, disjointedness to a want of proportion, incompleteness to a lack of orderly arrangement. These are the chief faults of the artist. These matters, however, can only be discussed with enlightened beings.

Some years ago I, Ssŭ, saw my father paint one or two pictures. Sometimes he put them away for ten and twenty days at a time, unfinished. As I think back on the matter, probably this was because he did not feel disposed to do them. Was not this disinclination the lazy spirit against which he spoke? When inspiration seized and won his mind, he would respond to its call and forget everything. Yet when a disturbance occurred, even though it were only a slight interruption, he would lay down his work and pay no further attention to it. Was not this distraction the cause of the confusion against which he spoke?

On a day when he was to paint, he would seat himself by a bright window, put his desk in order, burn incense to his right and left, and place good brushes and excellent ink beside him; then he would wash his hands and rinse his ink-well, as if to receive an important guest, thereby calming his spirit and composing his thoughts. Not until then did he begin to paint. Does this not illustrate what he meant by not daring to face one's work thoughtlessly? Having drawn a picture, he would retouch here and add there; augment and adorn it. If once would have been sufficient, he would go back to it for the second time. If twice would have been enough, he would go back to it the third time. Every circle he drew, he went over again to make it perfect. From beginning to end he worked as if he were guarding against a strong enemy. Does this not prove what he meant by painting without conceit in one's heart?

Indeed all our affairs, regardless of their greatness or smallness, should be executed in this manner. Then success may come to us at the end. My father repeated these teachings to me over and over again in one way or another, and I have followed them as principles throughout my life.

To learn to draw a flower, it is best to place a blossoming plant in a deep hollow in the ground and look down upon it. Then all its qualities may be grasped. To learn to draw bamboo, take a branch and cast its shadow on a white wall on a moonlight night; then its true outline can be obtained. To learn to paint landscape, too, the method is the same. An artist should identify himself with the landscape and watch it until its significance is revealed to him. The rivers and valleys of a fine landscape, viewed at a distance, show their contours; viewed at close range, they show their component parts.

The clouds and atmosphere of the real landscape are not the same throughout the four seasons. In spring they are bright and harmonious; in summer dense and brooding; in autumn thin and scattered; in winter dark and gloomy. When an artist succeeds in reproducing this general tone and not a group of disjointed forms, then clouds and atmosphere seem to come to life.

The mist and haze on the mountains are not the same either throughout the four seasons. The mountains of spring are tranquil and captivating as if they smiled; the mountains of summer are fresh and green as if they dripped with dew; the mountains of autumn are clean and neat as if beautifully ornamented and arrayed; the mountains of winter are melancholy and subdued as if in sleep. If in painting these mountains an artist observes the essential nature of his scene and does not follow details too closely, then the atmosphere or tone of the mist and haze will be justly reproduced.

The wind and rain of the actual landscape are best studied at a distance; at close range, the intricacies of their motions interfere with the artist's comprehension of the scene as a whole.

The clarity and cloudiness of the real landscape should be studied from a distant view. From near by the scene appears patched and cramped, and all distinctions between light and shade and the visible and the invisible are lost.

A man on the mountain gives a clue to a path; a pavilion on the mountain gives a clue to an excellent view; the woods of the mountain with their light and shade indicate the far and the near; the streams of the mountain, now continuous and now intercepted by ravines and valleys, mark the shallowness and the depth of the water; ferries and bridges indicate human activities; fishing boats and tackles indicate the purposes of men.

A great mountain is so stately that it becomes the master of multitudinous others arranged about it in order. It becomes the great master of the hills and slopes, forests and valleys, far and near, small and large. Its appearance is that of an emperor sitting majestically in all his glory, accepting the service of and giving audience to his subjects, without sign of arrogance or haughtiness.

A tall pine tree is so stately that it becomes a leader amongst the other trees. It stretches out accordingly over vines and creepers, grass and trees, a leader for those who are unable to support themselves. Its state is like that of a prince who wins the approval of his age and receives the services of lesser people, without sign of anxiety or vexation.

A mountain viewed at a close range has one appearance; a mountain viewed at a distance of several miles has another. When viewed from a distance of scores of miles, it has still another. The change of appearance caused by the varying degree of distance from the object is figuratively known as 'the change of shape with every step one takes'. The front view of a mountain has one aspect; the side view another; the back view still another. The ever changing view of the mountain from whatever side one looks is described as 'different shapes of a mountain as seen from every side'. Thus a single mountain combines in itself several thousand appearances. Should we not realize this fact?

Spring and summer views of the mountains have

certain aspects; autumn and winter views have others. That is to say the scenery of the four seasons is not the same. The morning view of the mountain has its own appearance; the evening view its own; views on a clear or cloudy day still their own. That is to say the morning and evening views of the mountains are not the same. Thus views of a single mountain combine in themselves the changes and significances of several thousand mountains. Should we not study them thoroughly?

The spring mountain is wrapped in an unbroken stretch of dreamy haze and mist, and men are joyful; the summer mountain is rich with shady foliage, and men are peaceful; the autumn mountain is serene and calm, with leaves falling, and men are solemn; the winter mountain is heavy with storm clouds and withdrawn, and men are forlorn.

The sight of such pictured mountains arouses in man exactly corresponding moods. It is as if he were actually in those mountains. They exist as if they were real and not painted. The blue haze and white path arouse a longing to walk there; the sunset on a quiet stream arouses a longing to gaze upon it; the sight of hermits and ascetics arouses a longing to dwell with them; rocks and streams arouse a longing to saunter among them. The contemplation of good paintings nourishes this longing. The places become real, and the meaning of these pictures is wonderful.

The mountains in the south-eastern part of the country are superbly beautiful, not because heaven and earth are partial to them, but because the land in that section is very low. Into it the waters pour and the streams flow, washing, cleansing, and changing it until they pass away leaving the soil thin and the water shallow. The mountains here are full of marvellous peaks and hanging cliffs, which reach far into the heavens. Waterfalls drop from the mists and the clouds like the cascades of the Hua-shan, which are almost a thousand feet high. Not that other falls are less than one thousand feet high, but that the mountains that equal the Hua-shan in richness are few, for although some rise from the surface, few rise from the heart of the earth.

The mountains in the north-western part of the country are rich and massive, not because heaven and earth are partial to them, but because the land in that section is very high. The rivers wind and swell among hills and banks, digging into the earth; the soil is thick and the water deep. The mountains piled with rolling, squatting mounds stretch forth thousands of miles in unbroken lines. The border hills are peaked, and, elegantly standing in the wilderness with their rugged tops, remind one of Shao Shih of the Sung-shan. Not that other peaks are not elegant, but that peaks like Shao Shih of the Sung-shan are rare, for they rise from the heart of the earth and not from the surface.

Characteristics of great Mountains

The Sung-shan is known for its beautiful streams; the Hua-shan for its elegant peaks; the Hêng-shan for its beautiful crevices; the Ch'ang-shan for its beautiful gorges; the T'ai-shan for its superb master peak. The Wu-i of the T'ien-t'ai, the Yen-tang of the Lu-huo, the Wu-hsia of the Min-o, the Wang-wu of the T'ien-t'an, and the Wu-tang of the Lin-lü are all famous mountains and store-houses of the world, in which are found the treasures of heaven and earth. In their caves the saints and hermits found the life of seclusion.

Indeed their unique forms and divine beauty are inexhaustible. Let one who wishes to portray these masterpieces of creation first be captivated by their charm; then let him study them with great diligence; let him wander among them; let him satiate his eyes with them; let him arrange these impressions clearly in his mind. Then with eyes unconscious of silk and hands unconscious of brush and ink, he will paint this marvellous scene with utter freedom and courage and make it his own.

This was exactly the same mood which took possession of Huai Su,[6] who, upon hearing the torrent of the river Chia-ling one night, made his grass writing still more beautiful, and Chang Tien,[7] who upon witnessing the master swordsmanship of Lady Kung Sun, was able to refine upon his brush work.

To-day, however, those who take up painting have

had no training of wide scope; they are confused and immature in what they see; they have had no wide practice; and they have no skill in selecting their subjects. Yet they obtain paper and clear the wall space, and immediately wave the brush and spread the ink. How can they ever hope to understand the landscape of haze and mist or convey the inspiration of streams and hills? The immaturity of young students results in numerous faults. What do we mean by a training of wide scope? Recently an artist painted a picture entitled: 'A virtuous man enjoying the mountains', in which he represented an old man gazing upon a mountain with his chin supported by the peak. There was another scroll entitled: 'A wise man enjoying the water', in which was represented an old man inclining his ears before the cascade. These examples illustrate the faults arising from the lack of wide scope in training. A virtuous man enjoying the mountains should be represented as in the scroll of the *Villa* by Po Lo-t'ien.[8] There the significance of living in the mountains is fully expressed. A wise man enjoying water should be represented as in the scroll of the *Wang Ch'uan* by Wang Mo-chieh.[9] There the delight in water is richly shown. Indeed, how can the enjoyment of virtuous and wise men be represented by a pose of a single figure?

What do we mean by clarity and maturity of

observation? The artists of to-day in painting mountains draw only three or five peaks; in drawing water only three or five ripples. This is due to the fault of immaturity. In drawing mountains there should be a great many. If the high and low, the small and large, those which turn their backs to each other, those which turn their fronts to each other, all merge harmoniously as if in mutual salutation, then the significant beauty of the mountains is expressed. In drawing water, if the peaceful, the raging, the whirling, the dashing, and the overflowing, are all portrayed; if the river is shown leading out towards a far expanse; then the representation of water is varied, and is abundant and satisfying in itself.

What do we mean by the lack of wide practice? The artists of the present day who have been brought up in the Chekiang and Kiangsu Provinces, are prone to paint the high barren landscape of the south-east; those who dwell in Shensi Province are apt to draw the magnificent billowy tops of the Kuan Lung; those who model their work upon that of Fan K'uan lack the refinement and charm of Ying Ch'iu; those who follow Wang Wei lack the strength of Kuan T'ung. Faults of this type are due to the lack of wide practice.

What do we mean by the lack of skill in selection? Mountains a thousand miles long are not striking, throughout their whole length; water stretching forth ten thousand miles is not superb in all its length. Although Mount T'ai-hang stretches over a large part of the kingdom, it looks most beautiful at the Lin-lü. The T'ai-shan dominates the ancient kingdoms of Ch'i and Lu, yet the most sublime scenery is at Mount Lung-yen. If the artist paints these mountains just as they are, the result will be no different from a map. Faults of this kind come from a lack of skill in selecting subjects.

Therefore, too much emphasis on the slopes and banks makes the work crude; too much emphasis on calm and quiet, trite; too much emphasis on human figures makes the work commonplace; too much emphasis on houses and arbors makes the work confused; too much emphasis on stones makes it bony; while too much emphasis on soil makes it fleshy.

A painting in which the brush-traces show too plainly has no unity and is coarse; coarse work has no true meaning. Work in which the ink shows no freshness of colour is arid; in arid work, there is no life. If water does not flow forward, then it is dead. If clouds do not move freely, then they are frozen. Mountains on which clear and dark spots are not distinguishable are without light and shade, while ones without visible and invisible parts are without mist and haze. Now the portion of a mountain on which the sun shines is bright, while the other portion where the sun does not fall is dark. Mountain shapes are dependent upon the light and the shade of the sun. Without sunlight there is no light and shade. Now that portion of a mountain which is covered with mist is invisible, while that other portion which is untouched by mist is visible. Aspects of the Mountains are dependent upon the absence or presence of mists. Without haze and mist there is no division of hidden or apparent parts.

A mountain is a large object: hence its form may be high and towering; it may stretch out proudly, stand in grandeur, crouch down, or slope forward; it may be majestic, energetic, austere, ingratiating, or obeisant; it may have a cover above or pedestal beneath; have some support in front or in back; it may look down as if to view the scene or march down as if to command. Such are the great form-aspects of the mountains.

Water is a living thing: hence its aspect may be deep and serene, gentle and smooth; it may be vast and ocean-like, winding and circling. It may be oily and shining, may spout like a fountain, shooting and splashing; it may come from a place rich in springs and may flow afar. It may form waterfalls rising up against the sky or dashing down to the deep earth; it may delight the fishermen, making the trees and grass joyful; it may be charming in the company of mist and clouds or gleam radiantly, reflecting the sunlight in the valley. Such are the living aspects of water.

Water-courses are the arteries of a mountain; grass and trees its hair; mist and haze its complexion. Therefore with water a mountain becomes alive; with grass and trees beautiful; with mist and haze charming and elegant. Water has the mountains as its face; arbors and terraces as its eyes and eye-brows; fishing and angling give it animation. Therefore with mountains, water becomes charming; with arbors and terraces bright and pleasing; with fishing and angling free and spacious. Such are the combinations of mountains and water.

Some mountains are high, while others are low. A high mountain has its arteries low. Its shoulders and thighs are broad and spreading; its foundations are thick and strong; and its peaks and cliffs stand close, supplemented by each other and connected in a continuous chain. Such indeed is the high mountain; it is said to be not solitary and not falling. A low mountain has its arteries higher up. Its peaks droop slightly; its neck and shoulders are closely connected; its root and base are broad and ponderous; its mounds are full and rounded. It reaches down straight to the earth, and no one can fathom its depth. Such indeed is the low mountain; it is said to be not shallow and not scattered. If a high mountain is solitary, it seems about to fall; if a low mountain is slight or lean, then its significance is dispersed. Such are the forms and relationships of mountains and water.

Stones are the bones of heaven and earth. Bones are valuable when they are buried deep and do not appear on the surface. Water is the blood of heaven and earth. Blood is valuable when it circulates and not when it congeals.

Mountains with no mist and clouds are like a springtime with no flowers and grass.

Mountains without clouds are not fair; without water not charming; without paths inactive; without trees and forests lifeless; without depth, they seem shallow; without an extension of space before them, they seem too close; without height, they seem too low.

A mountain has three dimensions: looking up to the top from below gives the dimension called height; looking toward the back from the front gives the dimension called depth; looking across at a mountain from an opposite height gives the horizontal dimension. The tone of the distance of height is clear and bright; that of depth, heavy and gloomy; that of the horizontal plane is sometimes clear and sometimes dark. Height is obtained by expressing an upward force. Depth is obtained by piling layer upon layer. The effect of distance is obtained by the use of misty lines which gradually disappear. In painting human figures in these three dimensions those of the heights must be clear and distinct; those in the depths detailed and fine; those in the distance dreamy and tranquil. Clear and distinct figures should not be short; fine and detailed ones not too tall; mild and dreamy ones not too large. These are the laws of the three dimensions.

Mountains have three degrees of magnitude. A mountain is larger than a tree, and a tree is larger than a man. If a mountain at a distance of several scores of miles does not have the size of a tree, then it is not a large mountain. If several thousand trees at several scores of miles do not have the size of a man, then they are not large trees. The part of a tree used in comparison with men is the leaves. The part of a man used in comparison with trees is the head. A few leaves correspond in size to a man's head, and a man's head to a few leaves. The size of men, of trees, and of mountains arise out of this category of proportions. These are the laws of magnitude.

If one wishes to paint a high mountain, one should not paint every part, or it will not seem high. When mist and haze encircle its waist, then it seems tall. If one wishes to paint a stream stretching afar, one should not paint its entire course, or it will not seem long. When its course is interrupted and shadowed, then it seems long. Indeed, a mountain shown in its entirety is not only without beauty, but it is as awkward as a picture of a rice mortar. A stream painted in its entire course is not only without grace in its meandering, but it resembles a drawing of an earth-worm.

Even though valleys, hills, forests, and trees in the foreground of a landscape painting may bend and curve, wind and meander with great elaboration, the scene will not tire the beholder with its many details, for the human eye has the power to grasp all the details in the foreground. Because of the open space of the plain at one side and the lines of the peaks vanishing, continuous as ocean waves in the horizon, the beholder will not weary of the distance; for human eyes can encompass a wide view.

A distant mountain has no wrinkles; distant water no waves; a man at a distance has no eyes. Not that they have none, but that they seem to have none.

The Meaning of Painting

(*Hua I*)

Although people know that I paint with a brush, little do they realize how difficult it is to paint. In the *Chuang-tzŭ* it is said that a painter at work 'took off his clothes and squatted down cross-legged'.[10] That is indeed the true way of the artist. He should nourish in his bosom cheerfulness and a happy mood. That is, if he can develop a natural, sincere, gentle, and honest heart, then he will immediately be able to comprehend the aspects of tears and smiles and of objects, pointed or oblique, bent or inclined, and they will be so clear in his mind that he will be able to put them down spontaneously with his paint brush.

It is said that Ku K'ai-chih of the Tsin dynasty always built a high pavilion as his place of painting. He was truly a man of wide vision in the ancient time. For, without such aids, an artist's thoughts become depressed, melancholy, or clogged, and he broods over some trivial matter. Then how can he paint the real forms of objects or express emotions? For example, an artisan wishing to make a harp finds a solitary dryandra from Mount I-yang.[11] Having skill and knowing the mysteries of his art, although the tree is still rooted in the ground and the leaves and branches still uncut he immediately has a clear mental picture of a finished lute. A master like Lei has that kind of eye for his material. But with troubled thoughts and a worn-out body a dull and insensitive man would see the pointed chisels and sharp knives before him and not know where to begin. Then how could he be expected to make 'a lute of half-burnt wood' which would have five mystic notes or would sound forth most delightfully with the clear wind and the flowing stream?

It has been said by the ancients that poetry is a picture without form, and painting is a poem with form. Philosophers often discoursed on this topic and it has been my guiding principle. In my leisure hours, therefore, I often perused the poetry of the Tsin and T'ang dynasties as well as the modern, and found that some of the beautiful lines give full expression to the inmost thoughts of men's souls, and describe vividly the scenery before men's eyes. Nevertheless, unless I dwell in peace and sit in leisure, with windows cleaned, the desk dusted, incense burning, and ten thousand worries drowned and subdued, I am not able to get at the mood and meaning of beautiful lines, think excellent thoughts, and imagine the subtle feelings described in them. The same thing is true of painting. It is not easy to grasp its meaning. When I am responsive and at one with my surroundings and have achieved perfect co-ordination of mind and hand, then I start to paint freely and expertly, as the proper standard of art demands. Men of to-day, however, are swept away by their impulses and feelings, and rush to complete their work.

Therefore, I, Ssŭ, have set down the following poems, some of which my father was fond of reciting. He considered that some of them contained themes appropriate for painting. To them I have added others which I have sought out for myself. I list them below.

Gazing at Mount Nu I

On the peak of Mount Nu I the spring snow is gone.
By the roadside apricot flowers begin to bud.
Not knowing when I can fulfil my heart's desire to depart,
In despair I turn back my carriage at the rustic bridge.

By YANG SHIH-E.

A Visit to a Mountain Retreat

Alone I set out to visit a mountain retreat, now stopping, now proceeding again.
Thatched cottages are linked behind the pine branches.
Though the host hears my voice, the gate is not yet open;
By the fence over the wild lettuce flutters a yellow butterfly.

By CH'ANG-SUN TSO-FU.

Some appropriate Themes

[*Thoughts on My Brother*]

When will my brother, sojourning in the south, return?
I only know he is among the Three Rivers and the Five Ranges.
Alone I stand at the Heng Gate and gaze over the immensity of the autumn waters wide;
A lone raven starts away, and the sun sets behind the mountain.

By Tou Kung.

After fishing I moor my lone boat among the reeds
And open a new bottle of wine and undo a package of preserved fish.
Since I became a fisherman on the banks of the Kiang and the Chê,
For twenty and more years my hands have never been folded in salutation.

Anon.

South of my house, north of my house, the spring is in flood;
Day after day I have seen only gulls . . .

By Tu Fu.

Crossing the stream, my lame mule straightens his ears;
Shunning the wind, my lean servant raises his shoulders.

By Lu Hsüeh.

I will walk till the stream ends
And sit to watch the clouds rise.

By Wang Mo-ch'i.

In the sixth month with a cane I come to a stony pass;
In the noon-tide shade, I hear a murmuring stream.

By WANG CHIEH-FU.

With a few creakings of the long oars,
  I depart from the shore;
With a few drippings of the water clock,
  I pass cities and mountains.

By WEI YEH.

Joining the sky, the distant water becomes crystal-like;
Half hidden in the heavy fog, the lone city wall looks immense.

By TU FU.

The dog sleeps under the shade of the flowers;
The cow grazes in the pasture amidst the rain.

By LI HOU-TS'UN.

The bamboo thicket sieves the rain drops;
The high peak holds the evening glow.

By HSIA-HOU SHU-CHIEN.

On the distant horizon an approaching goose appears small;
On the vast waters a departing ship seems forlorn.

By YAO HO.

Clouds wait brooding for snow and hang heavily over the earth;
The wail of autumn is uninterrupted as the wild geese sweep over the sky.

By CH'IEN WEI-YEN.

Appropriate Themes

Heavy with rain the spring flood rushes rapidly through the night;
Not a soul on the bank; a solitary ferry lies aslant the water.

By Wei Ying-wu.

Together we gazed on distant waters;
Alone I sit in a lone boat.

By Chang Ku.

Rules for Painting

(*Hua Chüeh*)

When you are planning to paint, you must create a harmonious relationship between heaven and earth. What do we mean by heaven and earth? Take for example a piece of silk a foot and a half long. The upper part must necessarily be the position of heaven, while the lower must be that of earth. The artist must arrange his ideas and design his scenery and fit them into the space between them. To-day, however, as I watch the beginners, they grasp their brush hurriedly, plan carelessly, and splash ink according to their impulses. One looks at their paintings and finds that the crowded details clog one's view and produce an unpleasant impression. How can such casual artists express the beauty of sublime and lofty sentiment?

In painting a landscape attention must first be given to the large mountain which may be called the master peak. When this is decided upon, other details come next: the perspective and proportion should be worked out in relation to the master peak, which will dominate the whole region—that is why it is called the master peak. Figuratively speaking, its relation to the others should be that of an emperor to his subjects, a master to his servants.

In painting stones and trees, the first consideration should be given to a large pine tree, which may be called the aged master. The aged master having been decided upon, an artist may proceed to the other details. For example, curious nests, small plants, little flowers, parasitic plants, and split stones all provide subsidiary details in the painting of a mountain. Hence the pine tree is called the aged master, and its relation to the others is that of a personage of high virtue to lesser man.

Some mountains are covered with earth, while others are covered with stones. If the earthy mountain has stones on top, then trees and forest growth will be scarce and lean, but if the stony mountain has earth on top, the vegetation will flourish. Some trees grow on a mountain, some trees beside the water. On a mountain where the soil is rich, there may grow a pine tree a thousand feet high. Beside water where the soil is lean, there may grow a shrub only a few feet high.

Some water flows; some stones are flat like slates. Some water forms cascades; some stones are curiously shaped. A waterfall jumps from the face of the forest; strangely shaped stones crouch by the roadside like tigers.

There is rain about to rain; there is snow about to

snow. There is heavy rain; there is heavy snow. There is the clearing of the rain; there is the clearing of the snow. There is the sudden gust of wind; there is the receding cloud. There is the great wind; there is the light fleeting cloud. The great wind has a force that makes the sand fly and the stones roll; the light cloud has the grace of a lovely maid clad in a thin veil.

An inn and hut stand by a ravine and not by a delta. They are in the ravine to be near the water; they are not by the delta because of the danger of flood. Even if some do stand by the delta, they are always in a place where there is no danger of flood . Villages are situated on the plain and not on the mountain, because the plain offers land convenient for cultivation, while hills are too far removed from arable land. Though some villages are built among the mountains, these are near to arable land among the hills.

Big pine trees and big stones must always be painted on great banks and great slopes, and not on shallow shoals and flat inlets.

A painter should be master over and not a slave to his brush. He should be master over and not a slave to his ink. Brush and ink are trivial things, but if an artist does not handle them with freedom, how can he be expected to attain to the heights of skill. Complete mastery is not very difficult to acquire. To take an example near at hand, we find a close analogy in calligraphy. It has been said that Wang Hsi-chih was fond of geese because of the easy and graceful movements of their necks which reminded him of the movements of a man holding a brush, who by using his forearm writes characters perfectly. This applies as well to the use of the brush in painting. It is generally true that men who are masters in calligraphy are also master painters. Both practise a free and unhesitating movement of the elbow in the employment of the brush.

I am asked what inks should be used.

I reply: there is burnt ink, preserving ink, receding ink, and the ink made of dust. One kind of ink is not sufficient; a single kind of ink cannot give the desired effect.

Of the ink-stones, those made of stone, pottery, earthenware or fragments of a broken water jar may be used. Of the inks one should use only those of high quality; not necessarily, however, the famous *Tung-ch'uan* or the *Hsi-shan.*

With regard to brushes, many kinds may be used: pointed, rounded, coarse, fine, needle-like, and broad ones.

With regard to ink, one may use sometimes light ink, sometimes dark, sometimes burnt ink, preserving or receding ink, sometimes ink made from kitchen soot, or ink mixed with dark blue. These inks are all mixed with water for use. Light ink retraced six or seven times, gives a dark colour the tone of which is rich and moist, and not dry or dead. Dark and burnt inks have their special uses. In drawing the outlines unless one uses them both, the curves of pine cones and the angles of rocks will not be clear. After the clear outlines are drawn, they are to be retraced with ink mixed with blue; then they appear always as if they had just come out of the mist and dew. The repeated use of light ink in a circling motion is called the touch of light ink. The use of the sharp-pointed brush horizontally in a backward and forward motion is called the smoothing of the wrinkles. The repeated rinsing of a drawing with water and ink is called making the colour stand out in relief. Bathing with water and ink well mixed is called cleansing. To work vertically with the tip of the brush is called hitting, while to work from top to bottom with the brush is called pulling. To drop and hold the point of the brush is called pointing. Pointing is used in drawing figures and also leaves. To draw the brush steadily backward is called drawing. This stroke is used in drawing turrets and pine needles. Light and shade on snow is produced by the use of heavy and light ink.

If only one kind of ink is used, the effect then is monotonous. The colour of mist is usually achieved by leaving the natural colour of the silk untouched. If, however, an artist wishes to make the mist stand out, he may use a light saturated ink, but neither ink nor brush strokes should ever be visible. The colour of wind can be achieved by the use of yellow clay or ink made of soot; the colour of earth by light or soot ink; the colour of stone by mixing blue with black ink, thus obtaining perspective. Waterfalls are shown by the natural colour of the silk. Only their sides are drawn with burnt ink.

Water is green in spring; jade green in summer; blue in autumn; and black in winter. The sky is bright in spring; azure in summer; clear in autumn; gloomy in winter. The room where the artist paints should be a wide and secluded chamber, warm in winter and cool in summer. The mind of a painter should not be disturbed by hundreds of worries; his spirit should be untroubled and joyful. In a poem by Tu Fu, this truth is revealed:

Painting only one stream in five days,
And only one stone in ten days;
Refusing to yield to compulsion and pressure,
Wang Tsai then was willing to hand down his master strokes.

There remain to be considered now the themes and subjects suitable for painting. There are four seasons, and each season in its turn has a beginning and an end.

The morning and evening, the moods of objects and the colours of things must all be analysed. Moreover, each has its characteristic mood. Aside from themes related to the four seasons, there are some incidents or stories taken either from classical, historical, or philosophical writings, which should be given due consideration in accordance with the vogue and taste of each particular period in turn.

Spring themes may be selected as follows: clouds of early spring; early spring rain; early spring with snow; clearing after the spring snow; clearing after the spring rain; a misty spring rain; chilly clouds of early spring about to turn into rain; an evening of early spring; sunrise over the spring mountains; spring clouds about to turn into rain; the mist and haze of early spring; spring clouds rising out of the valley; the dance of spring on the swollen stream; spring rain blown aslant by a spring wind; clear and beautiful spring mountains; a spring cloud like a white stork. These are all spring themes.

For summer these themes may be chosen: the lifting of the mists over the summer mountains; summer mountains after rain; wind and rain on summer mountains; morning walks in summer mountains; a forest retreat in summer mountains; a mountain ramble in summer rain; trees and forests in summer hills; curiously shaped stones; distant pines and stones on summer mountains; rain passing over summer mountains; clouds heavy with rain; a swift wind and sudden showers or a sudden wind and swift rain; a rainstorm ending over the summer mountains; returning of the clouds; dashing torrents after the summer rain; misty dawn over the summer mountains; misty twilight over summer mountains; a mountain retreat in summer; cumulus clouds in the summer sky. These are all summer themes.

For autumn: early autumn after rain; clearing after rain on an autumn plain; clearing of the autumnal sky; autumn wind after rain; a cloud descending over the autumn hills; autumn mist lifting out of the valley; autumn wind bringing rain. Or again: west wind bringing rain; autumn wind with misty rain; west wind with swift rain; mist and fog on an autumnal evening; evening over the autumn mountains; evening glow on the autumn hills; a plain on an autumn evening; clear water in the distance; autumn evening over a motley forest; forests and stones in autumn; stones and pine trees in an autumn scene; autumnal expanse. These are all autumn themes.

For winter: chilly clouds about to turn into snow; winter gloom heavy with snow; wind and drifting snow; light snow on the mountains and brooks; snow on distant streams; a mountain cottage after snow; a fisherman's hut in the snow; stopping the boat to obtain wine; a snowy walk to obtain wine; a snow-covered plain with a stream. Or again: wind and snow on the plain; snow-covered pine beside a deserted stream; snow intoxicated cottage among pines; wind whispering around a mill. These are all winter themes.

As to dawn: there is dawn in spring and in autumn; dawn in rain and in snow; dawn in mist and haze; dawn in autumn and spring. These are all themes of dawn.

As to evening, these themes may be chosen: evening glow on a spring mountain; evening glow after the rain; evening glow over the vestiges of snow; evening glow reflected over the river; evening glow on the distant water; evening mountains wrapped in mist and haze; a priest returning at dusk to a mountain temple; a guest arriving at the gate in the twilight. These are all themes of evening.

As to pine-trees, these themes are possible: twin pines; a group of three, five, or six; oddly-shaped pines; very ancient ones; old ones; others leaning against a bank; an old pine projecting from a cliff; some extremely tall pines. A pine-tree set on a peak is felicitous; it should be green and tall.

I once saw my father paint a pine-tree set on a distant mountain range. On the top of the painting he conveyed at a glance the continuity of existence. Below in the foreground he placed an old man who, in his pose of caressing the pine-tree, gazed far into the distance. The old man looked as if he had been put there by the God of Longevity.

As to stones, these are possible subjects: curiously shaped or smooth rounded ones. Pine-stones are used in combination with clouds over pine-trees; forest-stones in combination with trees and forests. The curiously shaped Ch'iu Chiang stones are found in autumn on the banks of rivers. A spray or two of knot-weeds and reeds drawn on the bank of a river will give to a painting a suggestion of distance and so establish perspective.

As to clouds, these are possible subjects: clouds lying over the mouth of the valley; clouds rising out of the cliffs; white clouds rising over mountain ridges; light clouds descending from the peaks.

As to mist, these are possible subjects: mist lying over the mouth of the valley; mist rising out of the mountains; evening mist over the forests of the plain; a trailing light mist; mist over the hills in spring; haze over the hills in autumn.

As to water, these are possible subjects: a rushing stream; water dashing among pine-trees and rocks; a cascade from high mountain peaks; a waterfall in rain or snow; a waterfall in mist; distant water among the betel-nut trees; a fishing boat on a misty stream.

As to miscellaneous themes, these are possible: fishermen's cottages by the water; plowing viewed from a balcony; geese alighting on the plain; a wine shop by the bridge; a woodcutter on the bridge. These are only a few of the possible miscellaneous themes.

Notes

[1] The three *fên* probably appeared in one of the two lost books of the *Book of Changes.* Not a single trace of what they signify remains.

[2] One of the legendary emperors to whom is ascribed a form of picture writing which took the place of an earlier system of tying knots.

[3] Statesmen and nobles who retired to the mountains because their consciences would not allow them to serve sovereigns who were usurpers.

[4] A descendant of the T'ang dynasty emperors. He is often spoken of as Li Ying-ch'iu from the name of his birthplace in Shantung Province, and is one of the most important landscape painters of the early Northern Sung dynasty.

[5] A famous poet and essayist of the 8th century.

[6] A noted calligrapher of the T'ang dynasty whose grass writing set a high standard in that branch of art.

[7] Another calligrapher of the same period. Under the influence of artistic inspiration and wine he was often forgetful of decorum and came to be known as Chang the Madman.

[8] Po Chü-i, 772–846, one of the greatest poets of China.

[9] Wang Wei, the most famous landscape artist not only of the T'ang dynasty but of all periods. He built for himself a home on the banks of a small mountain stream in Shansi Province and gave it the name Wang Ch'uan.

This home of Wang Wei is famous for two reasons: it was the subject of one of his best poems and the name of one of his most brilliant paintings.

[10] The story is told that several artists were summoned before Prince Yuan of the Sung Court to paint a picture. Many presented themselves early and began at once to paint before the Prince. One artist, however, came late, made an obeisance, and then went off home. The Prince was curious about him and sent a man to see what he did. The messenger reported, 'He took off his clothes and squatted down cross-legged.'

'He will do,' cried the Prince. 'He is a true artist.'

[11] This story refers to a virtuoso and musician, T'sai Yung, of the second century. Once he came upon a peasant burning a piece of dryandra. Recognizing the marvellous quality of the wood by its peculiar crackle, he took the charred piece and fashioned from it his celebrated lute.